A Character Building Book™

Learning About Assertiveness from the Life of
Oprah Winfrey

Kristin Ward

The Rosen Publishing Group's
PowerKids Press™
New York

For Mike

Published in 1999 by The Rosen Publishing Group, Inc.
29 East 21st Street, New York, NY 10010

First Edition

Book Design: Erin McKenna

Photo Credits: p. 4 © Popperfoto/Archive Photos; p. 7 © David Allen/Corbis-Bettmann; p. 8 © Corbis-Bettmann; p. 11 © Richard Pasley/Corbis-Bettmann; p. 12 © King/The Gamma Liaison Network; p. 15 © Reuters/photographer unknown/Archive Photos; p. 16 © Jason Trigg/Archive Photos; p. 19 © Pacha/Corbis-Bettmann; p. 20 © M. Gerber/Corbis-Bettmann.

Ward, Kristin.
    Learning about assertiveness from the life of Oprah Winfrey / by Kristin Ward.
        p.   cm. — (A character building book)
    Includes index.
    Summary: A brief biography of the successful entertainer, Oprah Winfrey, focusing on the value of assertiveness.
    ISBN 0-8239-5348-3
    1. Winfrey, Oprah—Juvenile literature. 2. Television personalities—United States—Biography.—Juvenile literature. 3. Motion picture actors and actresses—United States—Juvenile literature. 4. Assertiveness (Psychology)—Juvenile literature. [1. Winfrey, Oprah. 2. Television personalities. 3. Actors and actresses. 4. Afro-Americans—Biography. 5. Women—Biography. 6. Assertiveness.] I. Title. II. Series.
PN1992.4.W56W37 1998
791.45'028'092—dc21   98-25136
[B]   CIP
                                                                                                              AC

Manufactured in the United States of America

Contents

Assertiveness in Action

Oprah Winfrey hosts a TV talk show that people watch all around the world. Oprah owns the **production studio** (proh-DUK-shun STOO-dee-oh) where her talk show, and other movies, are made. She is also a TV and movie actress and **producer** (pruh-DOO-ser).

Oprah is not afraid to be **assertive** (uh-SER-tiv). She is bold enough to say and do what she thinks is right.

◄ *Oprah has been successful in life because she is honest and assertive.*

Growing Up

Oprah was born on January 29, 1954, on her grandmother's farm in Mississippi. When she was six, Oprah went to live with her mother in Wisconsin. Oprah was very assertive in school. In fact, when she was bored in kindergarten she wrote her teacher a note asking to move to first grade. The teacher agreed that Oprah was ready and moved her to a first-grade class.

As she got older, Oprah started getting into trouble. She was sent to live with her father in Tennessee. Her dad was **strict** (STRIKT). He taught Oprah to behave at home and in school.

When Oprah was growing up she was too ▶
poor to wear fancy dresses like this one.

Working Hard

While Oprah went to college, she had a job too. She worked as a **reporter** (ree-POR-ter) at a radio station. During college Oprah decided that she wanted to be on television. She got a job on a news show. The news stories were written for her. Oprah just had to read them on TV. But she wanted to be on a show where she could do more than that.

Oprah got a new job on a talk show. She liked this better than the news. And people liked that Oprah said and did what she wanted.

The first talk show that Oprah worked on was called People Are Talking. *It was on television in Baltimore, Maryland.*

Taking a Risk

In 1986 a TV station in Chicago invited Oprah to host her own talk show. The show would be on at the same time as another popular talk show. Oprah was scared that the host of the other show might be better than she was. A friend reminded Oprah to be assertive. Oprah went to Chicago to **interview** (IN-ter-vyoo) for the job. Oprah told the producers that she would be **candid** (KAN-did) on TV. The producers liked Oprah's honest style and she got the job. It was a big step in Oprah's career.

On her show Oprah often goes into the audience with her microphone to talk to people. ▶

Being Famous

Oprah's talk show, called *The Oprah Winfrey Show*, has been on TV since 1986. She has won lots of awards for hosting it. Oprah is also asked to act in and produce movies. Her first movie was *The Color Purple* in 1985. Oprah also chooses stories that she would like to make into movies.

Being famous is exciting, but it can also be hard. Oprah has to be assertive about which projects she wants to do and how to do them.

Oprah has won many awards for her work in television and movies, including a People's Choice Award, in 1997.

Speaking Up

Oprah has worked hard to make her show different from other talk shows. Some talk shows are about silly or **sensational** (sen-SAY-shuh-nul) topics. On her show, Oprah talks to guests about serious issues. She wants her **viewers** (VYOO-erz) to see that lots of people have the same problems. Oprah wants the show to help guests and viewers solve their problems.

Oprah is assertive about picking the topics for her show. She always gives her opinion about what should and should not be done.

Oprah likes to have well-known, interesting people, such as First Lady Hillary Rodham Clinton, on her show. ▶

Making a Difference

Oprah is a popular talk show host, actress, and producer. She has also worked with people who have written books about her, and she's made a home video. She earns a lot of money from her work. She uses some of the money to help good causes. Oprah especially wants to help families. She wants children to be safe, and to have good lives. Oprah also wants to help grown-ups be good parents. Oprah helps families get the **resources** (REE-sor-sez) they need to make good lives for themselves.

◀ *Oprah has made a difference in many people's lives.*

Taking Care of Herself

Oprah is a very busy person, but she has learned that taking care of herself and staying healthy is important. Even when she travels for work, Oprah is assertive about taking time for herself. She makes sure that she always has time to eat right and exercise.

Oprah works with food and exercise **specialists** (SPEH-shuh-lists) who help her to stay healthy. Sometimes Oprah runs in races. She has even run a **marathon** (MAR-uh-thon)!

When Oprah finishes a race, she is tired but happy and proud of herself. ▶

Assertiveness on TV

Millions of people watch Oprah's show every day. A lot of people listen to Oprah because she is assertive and honest. When people talk about a problem on the show, Oprah listens to them and tries to help. She treats her guests like friends. Sometimes Oprah has had the same problem as a guest. And she's not afraid to tell them. Oprah knows that what she says can **influence** (IN-floo-ents) a lot of people. For example, Oprah has influenced her viewers to read books and to donate time and money to good causes.

◀ *Oprah uses her fame to inspire other people to take care of themselves.*

Role Model

Oprah has been assertive in her own life. She has learned to tell herself and others that she has **value** (VAL-yoo). Oprah speaks up and tells people what she thinks is right. And she wants to help other people to be bold and **self-confident** (SELF-KON-fih-dent) in their lives too.

Being assertive has helped Oprah to become who she wants to be in her life. She has fame, fortune, health, and the power to make a difference in other people's lives.

Glossary

assertive (uh-SER-tiv) Being self-confident and forceful in a positive way

candid (KAN-did) To be honest and sincere.

influence (IN-floo-ents) To have an effect on someone or something.

interview (IN-ter-vyoo) A meeting to figure out if a person has the right skills to do a job.

marathon (MAR-uh-thon) A road race that is 26.2 miles long.

producer (pruh-DOO-ser) A person who makes movies and TV shows.

production studio (proh-DUK-shun STOO-dee-oh) A place where movies and TV shows are made.

reporter (ree-POR-ter) A person who tells people the news.

resource (REE-sors) Knowledge or a material needed to do something.

self-confident (SELF-KON-fih-dent) Having faith in oneself.

sensational (sen-SAY-shuh-nul) Designed to excite or interest a person quickly.

specialist (SPEH-shuh-list) A person who has special skills and knowledge for doing something.

strict (STRIKT) To make sure other people follow your rules very carefully.

value (VAL-yoo) The worth and importance of something.

viewer (VYOO-er) A person watching a program, such as a TV show.

Index

DC

2013